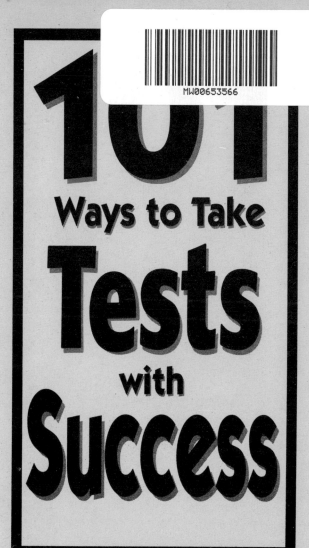

101
Ways to Take
Tests
with
Success

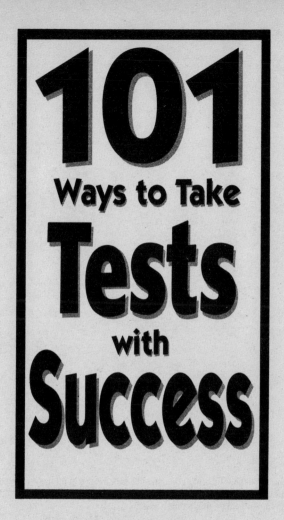

101
Ways to Take
Tests
with
Success

by **Denise Bieniek**

illustrated by **Aija Janums**

If you purchased this book without a cover, you should be aware that this book is stolen property. It was reported as "unsold and destroyed" to the publisher, and neither the author nor the publisher has received any payment for this "stripped book."

Text and illustrations copyright © 1997 by Troll Communications L.L.C.

ll rights reserved. No part of this book may be reproduced or utilized in any form or by any means, ronic or mechanical, including photocopying, recording, or by any information storage and al system, without written permission from the publisher.

he United States of America.

6 5 4 3 2 1

To all those who have ever had to take a test

Contents

Chapter 1
Always Be Prepared!   9

Chapter 2
The Best You Can Be   13

Chapter 3
The Road to Success:
Making the Most of Your Time in School   25

Chapter 4
The Fork in the Road:
Making Choices on Your Own   33

Chapter 5
Practice Makes Perfect   45

Chapter 6
It's Show Time!   57

Chapter 7
All Kinds of Tests   65

Chapter 8
Don't Let Your Guard Down   79

Appendix   82

Bibliography   88

Index   89

Chapter 1
✓
Always Be Prepared!

✎✐✎✐✎✐✎✐✎✐✎✐✎✐✎

When you hear the word "test," what is your first reaction? Sweaty palms? Pounding heart? Panic? Do you ever wonder why everyone else in your class seems calm and collected while you are having an anxiety attack? Chances are your classmates are nervous about the test, too. But they may feel more confident than you do. You could ask your classmates what their secrets to being calm and relaxed are . . . or you can begin reading this book right now and learn how to face every test from now onward with confidence.

Why do you think your parents and teachers put pressure on you to do well? There are lots of reasons. Without good grades, you will have little chance of getting into a good college. Competition is fierce, and only those students who work hard will earn places in the most prestigious schools. Without a good college education, you won't have nearly as many opportunities for a rewarding and interesting career. And without a good career, you will not be able to afford the things you want most for yourself and your family.

Is that thinking a bit too far ahead? Okay, then think about this: How did you feel the last time you got a really great grade on a test? Pretty good, right? Well, you can have that feeling *every* time you take a test by following the guidelines in this book.

Take a minute to look at the table of contents at the front of this book. You will notice that the chapters are arranged chronologically from the time a test is scheduled to the day you sit down to take the test. You will be guided step by step through a series of techniques that have been designed to help you maximize your study time. By following the 101 tips in this book, you will be able to balance study time with sports and other activities without having to cram the night before a test.

Best of all, as you practice the techniques in this book and take the time to study properly, you will see your test scores improve. As your confidence in your test-taking abilities increases, you may even begin to feel less anxious about taking tests.

One more thing to consider. You will be faced with various types of tests throughout your life, even when your schooling is complete. Having the know-how to deal with tests as they arise is a super lifetime skill. Preparing yourself now will help you form habits that will serve you all your life. Let's get started!

Chapter 2
✓
The Best You Can Be

1. The key to a healthy mind is a healthy body. Remember to eat foods that are good for you. Before putting food into your body, ask yourself if you are eating something that is healthy. Sure, a candy bar tastes great and may give you quick energy. But the energy will be used up just as quickly and you'll feel sluggish the rest of the day. Foods that will be used up by your body slowly and efficiently, like bread, pasta, and proteins, are the best foods for your body and brain.

This chart shows the various food groups. Next to each group is the recommended number of servings you should eat from that group each day. Does your diet come close?

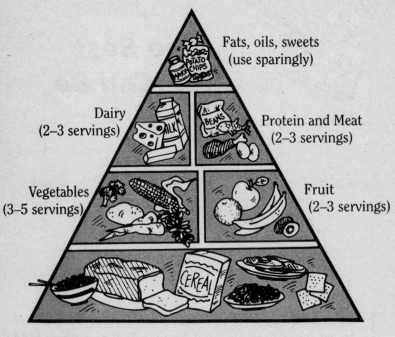

Fats, oils, sweets
(use sparingly)

Dairy
(2–3 servings)

Protein and Meat
(2–3 servings)

Vegetables
(3–5 servings)

Fruit
(2–3 servings)

Grains
(5–11 servings)

2. Get plenty of sleep each night. A growing body needs sleep as much as food. Figure out how much sleep *your* body needs to function smoothly the next day. The chart shows the amount of sleep you should aim for each night—especially the night before a test!

Age	Recommended Hours of Sleep (approximate)
6–12 yrs.	10 hours
12–16 yrs.	8.5 hours
16–22 yrs.	7–8 hours

3. Besides eating well and getting plenty of sleep, your body needs regular exercise. If you exercise at least three times a week for about twenty minutes each time, your brain will be more alert, your body will be stronger and more agile, and you will feel better. Try going for a brisk walk, shooting baskets with a friend, or joining a school sports team.

4. NEVER TAKE DRUGS! Sometimes people take drugs before a test because they think the drugs will calm them down or keep them awake. But drugs won't help you—in fact, it is much more likely that you will do worse on a test. Drugs and alcohol also destroy brain cells and alter your senses. The only "safe" drugs are those your doctor prescribes for you—and even those should be taken only with care and with adult supervision.

5. Discover your inner time clock. Are you full of energy in the morning and worn out by 8:00 at night? Or are you the type of person who has to be dragged out of bed in the morning but has lots of energy at night? Spend a few days analyzing when you do your best work. Plan to study during your prime time to get the maximum benefits from your study efforts. You will work better and more efficiently when you are alert and ready to study.

6. Learn to schedule your time. You'll be able to get everything done and you'll feel less pressured. You may even find you have time left over for a special activity! Follow these guidelines for creating a personal schedule:

- For the next few days, write down *everything* you do and the time you spend doing each activity.

- Even if you are doing nothing, write it down. At the end of the week, tally up the time you spent doing each activity.

- Can you make better use of your time? Try reorganizing your time so there will be room for studying each day. Remember your inner time clock—schedule study time when you will be at your peak.

7. Create a weekly planner and write down every commitment and study session you have for each week. This way you will be able to remember everything, and if you need to make changes to your schedule, you will be able to do it quickly and efficiently. You can do your weekly planner on the computer. If you don't have a computer, make a master planner and photocopy it BEFORE you fill it in. Make enough copies for the school year (and for next year, too). If you prefer, you can buy a planner with printed weekly and monthly schedules at a stationery store.

8. Use your weekly planners to create a monthly planner. Jot down all important due dates and upcoming tests, plus any activities you have that will take away precious study time. Place the monthly planner in a highly visible spot, such as on top of your desk at home. Refer to the planner every few days to keep on top of your tests and assignments.

Weekly Planner

Date: *March 11*	English	Science	Soc. Studies	Math	Geography	Language
Monday	Read 3 or more chapters of *Gulliver's Travels*	Read chapter 6 and answer questions	Current Events Finish project for Wednesday	Review angles for test	Quiz on map of Europe	Study verbs "to be" and "to have"
Tuesday	Finish *Gulliver's Travels* for Wednesday discussion	Research topic due Friday—start thinking	Chapter 20 and questions	Geometry test	Go to library for research paper	Study for quiz. Finish oral report
Wednesday	Do outline for report. Study for quiz on *Gulliver's Travels*	Bring in examples of food groups	Project due on homes around the world	Do page 59 and questions 1–10	Call Phil for study date	Quiz on chapter 21 vocabulary
Thursday	Quiz. Write rough draft of report.	Write outline for research topic	Chapter 21 and questions			Oral report on foods of France
Friday	Rewrite report for Monday	Hand in outline for research topic	Choose partners for cooperative learning group	Review quiz	Current events	No class!

9. Create your own study place. This is where you will do your homework, make up your schedule for each week, study for tests, and keep all your important papers. The study place should be:

- **Free of distractions.** Try to find the quietest place in your house. Make sure there are no radios, televisions, or telephones nearby. If you study in your bedroom, remove any magazines, sports equipment, or projects that might distract you. If there is no quiet place in your house, find a quiet corner at your local library.

- **Comfortable.** If you study best at a desk or table, make sure one is available. Put your favorite chair at your desk. If you like to read on the floor, clear an area. You may want to scatter some pillows to lie on or lean on.

- **Appropriately sized.** If you have a small work area and your computer takes up most of the room, you'll spend too much time juggling books and papers. Make sure you have enough space to spread out your study materials so you can see as much as possible at a glance.

10.
Keep your study place well-stocked with items you will need when you study. Organize your study space so you know exactly where everything is. If your work area is messy, you'll waste valuable time searching for things.

11. If you need special materials, such as reference books, to prepare for a test, be sure to obtain them in advance. Call up your local library or bookstore to see if they have what you need as soon as you receive an assignment. Give yourself plenty of time to do the additional reading and absorb all the information.

12. Create a "Studying—Please Do Not Disturb!" sign for your door. Show it to your family, and explain that you will be using the sign whenever you are preparing for tests. Ask your family to respect your privacy when you are studying. Don't forget to hang the sign up before each study session!

13. Make a goal chart for yourself. Write down each subject and the grades you received on your last report card. Then write down what grades you will aim for on your next report card. Set reasonable—but challenging —goals for yourself.

Subject	Grade Last Term	Grade This Term
English	C+	B–
Math	C	C+
Social Studies	B	B+
Geography	B	B+
Science	B+	A!

14. Review your goal chart with your parents. Explain to them why you think your goals are reasonable and discuss any concerns or advice that they might have about how you can achieve your goals.

15. If you find that you are still not managing your time well, ask a parent to help you figure out a better way to schedule your work and play. An adult can often point out which areas should be adjusted or make arrangements to lighten your extracurricular activities. Don't procrastinate if you think there is a problem. The only person who can make a difference in your grades is you!

16. Remember—*You* are the best person to decide which methods work for you and which methods don't. Find out what works for you and practice every day.

Chapter 3

✓

The Road to Success: Making the Most of Your Time in School

❧ ✏ ❧ ✏ ❧ ✏ ❧ ✏ ❧ ✏ ❧ ✏ ❧

17. Pay attention in class! Your teacher's job is to share important information with you, and it is your job to listen to and understand the information being presented. If you find it hard to focus on the teacher because of distractions where you sit, ask to be moved. Sit with other students who want to listen and learn. If you have special needs, such as poor eyesight or hearing, let your teacher know about them so he or she can make sure to seat you in the proper place. It's up to you to create the best learning environment for your particular needs.

18. Find a Study Buddy. Ask someone who generally does well if he or she would exchange phone numbers with you. This way, if you miss a class and need the homework, your Study Buddy can give it to you. Or, if something is not clear in your notes, you can give your Study Buddy a call and discover just what those odd-looking words say. You and your Study Buddy can also get together before important exams to trade notes and ideas, and to motivate each other to learn.

19. Ask your teacher if he or she can give you any advice about how to improve your study habits and test scores. Be prepared to discuss the steps you take when doing homework and studying for tests. Your teacher will probably have lots of suggestions that will help. Make sure to write down what the teacher says and ask him or her to explain if anything is unclear. After you've tried some of the suggestions, follow up with your teacher to let him or her know if the suggestions were helpful. Your teacher will appreciate your efforts to improve your grades, and you will be rewarded with better study habits and better test results.

20. Learn to take notes that are clear and simple. Before writing anything down, try to decide what information is important and what is not. Write down only the important information. You may need to shorten words and phrases to make sure you have time to write all the information down. Follow these general guidelines for note-taking.

- Write only the beginning letters of words. For example, you might write "ans" for answer, "Dec of Ind" for Declaration of Independence, and "env" for environment.

- Write only the consonants in words and delete silent letters. For example, you might write "Grk mthlgy" for Greek mythology.

- Use symbols for words whenever possible. For example, write a question mark instead of the word "question." You'll find a list of common symbols on page 83 of this book.

- Abbreviate whenever possible. Look at page 84 for a list of common abbreviations.

- Above all, make sure you can read what you've written. What good are notes if you can't understand what they say?

21. Practice taking notes at home to help improve your shorthand skills. Ask a parent to read aloud a section from one of your textbooks. Try to write down the important information using the shorthand techniques described in tip #20. Then review your notes with your parent and see what you can do to improve your skills. Continue to practice at home every few days until you are comfortable and have come up with your own shorthand method of taking notes.

22. Write on only one side of each sheet of paper. Use the reverse side to add anything you may have missed while the teacher was speaking, or any additional information from your reading.

23. If you have a thought about something the teacher is saying while you are taking notes, make an "idea box." Write your idea or question in a box in the margin of your paper. If there is time, ask your question before class ends. If time runs out, look up information about your thought when you review your notes later that day. If something is not clear, have a follow-up question ready for the teacher the next day.

idea box   Did the war end in 1776?

George Washington was the first pres. of the U.S.

He was commander-in-chief of the col. army during the Rev. War.

24. Listen for clues from the teacher about important parts of a study unit. If the teacher says something like, "This was the turning point of the war" or "You will have to know this for your exam," make sure you highlight that information in your notes. Use a check mark, a star, or a big arrow to show which items the teacher has mentioned as particularly important. Spend extra time studying these points until you are sure you know all the information.

25. If a teacher gives an example of a question, write it down exactly as stated. There is a good chance that this question will appear on a test.

26. Carefully place your notes in order in the appropriate section of your notebook. When you review your notes later, everything will be in its proper place and you will not waste time organizing information.

27. Write your name at the top of all handouts from class. Use a three-hole punch so that you can place each handout in your notebook in the appropriate place. If you use a spiral notebook, staple or clip additional information to the back of the page with the appropriate notes.

28. Write down all assignments as soon as possible. Make sure you copy everything word for word. If you are not clear about something, ASK! After all, it's not very smart to spend time working on the wrong assignment.

29. If you do not understand something during class, be sure to stay and speak to the teacher when class is over. Fill in the information in the appropriate place in your notes. When you review your notes later that day, make sure you understand the concept.

30. When a test is announced, write the date in your assignment book and then on your monthly and weekly planners. Ask the teacher what material will be on the test. If possible, find out what kind of test it will be— true or false, essay, multiple choice, fill-in, or short answer.

31. Make sure you know if students will be permitted to use reference materials, books, or notes during the exam. Don't forget to ask your math teacher if you are allowed to bring a calculator for a math exam. Use the checklist on the next page to help you prepare for each test.

✔ Checklist

Subject_____Test Date _____

Teacher_____Test Room _____

Material on test _____

_____

_____

Things to bring to test:

☐ pen
☐ pencil
☐ ruler
☐ calculator
☐ dictionary
☐ thesaurus
☐ formulas
☐ protractor/compass
☐ outline
☐ textbook
☐ notes

Other _____

Chapter 4

✓

The Fork in the Road: Making Choices on Your Own

32. Don't procrastinate. If you have an important test on a Monday, don't put off studying for it until Sunday night. Start studying after school on Friday, then study a little on Saturday and more on Sunday. If you are studying for a midterm or a final exam, it may be helpful to make a chart outlining all the topics that will be covered on the test. You can then divide your time among all topics to make sure you know all the material.

33. Schedule study and review sessions on a regular basis. Remember, doing a good job on your homework is the best way to review the work you have done in class—and to find out where you may need help. When you are preparing for a big test, it may be helpful to have extra study sessions with your Study Buddy.

34. Find someone who knows the subjects you are studying and who is willing to share his or her expertise. Having someone around who can explain how to plot points on a graph, for instance, can really make your study time go a lot smoother than sitting there guessing. A brother or sister, parent, or your Study Buddy can make a great tutor.

35. Do your homework on time and completely. If you cannot do a particular assignment, or are unable to complete it, tell your teacher privately at the start of class. Then make up the assignment as soon as possible.

36. Review your notes every day.

- Reread your class notes. Reading them aloud will help you remember them better.

- Rewrite anything that is not clear. Call your Study Buddy if you do not understand a concept.

- Cross out any information that is not important. Sometimes when you are taking notes you take down insignificant information. Use this review time to pick out the most important points the teacher discussed in class. Rewrite your notes if necessary.

37. Use a highlighter to mark the most important words, dates, names, locations, and phrases in your notes. If you own your textbooks, you may wish to use this technique for reading assignments. Do not highlight as you are reading. Read through the assignment once, then go back and pick out only the most important information to highlight.

38. If your textbooks don't belong to you, jot down notes from your reading as you go along. Make sure that your notes are clearly written and that you understand the concept being discussed in your textbook. Afterward, outline what you have read in your study notebook.

39. When reading assignments in textbooks, be sure to read the introductions. This part of the text summarizes what that section of the book will discuss. Also, pay careful attention to the sentences or words that are written in bold. The bold text is always important and often provides a useful outline for the chapter or section.

40. At the end of each section of a textbook, there may be a list of questions about the chapter. Even if your teacher has not assigned the questions as homework, try to answer them on your own. This will give you a good indication of how well you understood the assignment you just read. You can also make up your own questions and ask a parent or your Study Buddy to quiz you.

41. Review your weekly and monthly study planners each day. Try to look ahead to see which days and weeks will be particularly busy. For example, if you are playing a sport and know that you have a lot of practices and games scheduled during a week when you have two tests, start preparing way in advance for these exams.

42. Use mnemonic devices to help you remember your notes. Mnemonic devices are tricks for recalling information.

- Make up rhymes. For example, "In fourteen hundred ninety-two, Columbus sailed the ocean blue."

- Draw pictures illustrating the most significant information.

- Make up number codes. How many numbers are in the date you need to remember? Think up a phrase having words with the same number of letters as the numbers in the date. Each word must have the same number of letters as the number it is representing. Example: You could use the phrase "I practiced piano endlessly" to remember the year Alaska and Hawaii were admitted to the Union (1959).

- Make up codes to remember a series of words, names, locations, and other facts.

- Jog your memory by using the first letter of each word you are trying to remember in a phrase or term. Example: You can remember the correct order of the planets of our solar system by memorizing this sentence:
My Very Excited Mother Just Sold Uncle Ned Pies (Mercury, Venus, Earth, Mars, Jupiter, Saturn, Uranus, Neptune, Pluto)

43. Several other mnemonic devices, such as Venn diagrams, songs, and mindmaps can help you remember your notes and classwork. Venn diagrams can help you visualize information. For example, let's say you were trying to memorize some of the more important gods in Greek and Roman mythology. Your Venn diagram would look something like this:

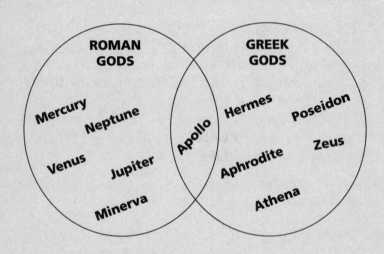

You will notice that the god Apollo was important to both the Greeks and the Romans. When you look over your notes to prepare for the test on this material, you will quickly remember this information.

Mindmaps help you organize lots of information into an easy-to-remember outline. Perhaps you have spent several weeks learning about plants—how they grow, how they reproduce, which plants live in which climates. Your head is spinning with all this information, and your notes are threatening to take over your entire notebook. You go through your notes, highlight the main topics, and make a mindmap that looks like this:

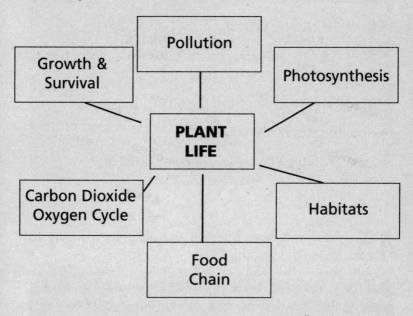

Now you have all the important points in one handy reference. When you are tested on this material, jot the mindmap down at the top of your test paper and refer to it as you answer the test questions.

44. Learn how to scan material. You can get more out of reading your textbook if you scan each chapter first.

Scanning Tips

• Read the chapter questions to help you focus on the key ideas in the chapters.

• Read the chapter heading and all subheadings.

• Read the first paragraph of the chapter and the first paragraphs under each subheading.

• Read the first sentences of the other paragraphs.

• Read the chapter summary.

• Look at all the illustrations, graphs, and charts.

45. After you have scanned the chapter, it's time to tackle the reading.

• Do not read the whole chapter by quickly turning page after page. Read one paragraph at a time at a comfortable reading rate. If you read too quickly, you may miss some important information.

• After reading each paragraph, think about what the author was trying to say. If you are completely lost, make a note to ask your teacher to explain the concept to you.

46. After reading each page, jot down the most important facts—dates, names, locations, new vocabulary, and events. Make sure you write down the page and paragraph you took your notes from in case you need to go back and check something later on.

47. The last step in textbook reading is to recall the information you have written down. Read the first few words of the notes for each paragraph and see if you can recall the key concepts from memory. If you cannot remember, go back to the paragraph and scan it for the information you need. You will have to practice this technique for a while before you can easily recall information. Don't get discouraged—and don't give up! All your hard work will pay off with better grades.

48. In your study place, keep a chart graphing your test grades. It will help you to see how well you are doing and what areas may need more time and attention.

49. Keep quizzes, tests, and other class papers in files in your study place. Use a system to sort out your papers. Many students find that dividing the papers by subject area is the best idea. Put the most recent papers at the front of the file. This way, when you look for something from the beginning of the year, you will know to search at the back of the file, and the more recent information will be available as soon as you open the file.

50. After you have taken one or more tests given by a particular teacher, look them over carefully and try to analyze them. Each teacher usually has a particular style of asking questions.

If you can figure out your teacher's style, keep it in mind when you begin studying for your next test. When you come across an important concept, think, "How would my teacher ask about this information?"

Your teacher may also use special tricks or distractions on his or her exams. Perhaps your teacher likes to put one outrageous answer in every multiple choice question. Or maybe he/she likes to make two answers very similar. If you take a few minutes to study your previous tests, you'll be able to pick out these tricks on your next test—and ace it!

Chapter 5

✓

Practice Makes Perfect

51. *Never* cram for a test. As any student who has crammed for a test can tell you, it doesn't work! Cramming for tests leaves you confused, panicked, and exhausted. And if you think about it, it's impossible to do your best on a test when you did not sleep the night before.

Make time in your schedule each week to review your textbook and class notes. You will have a much better chance of remembering the material correctly if you take the time to leisurely review the important concepts. And you will do better on the test if you get a good night's sleep the night before.

52. Organize your study materials so you won't have to keep stopping to look for things.

Get Organized

- Get out all the papers, quizzes, notes, and homework assignments that you will need before you begin studying.

- Make sure pens are handy, pencils are sharpened, and plenty of paper is available.

- Let everyone in the family know you are studying and cannot be disturbed. Find the quietest place in your house, make sure you have adequate lighting, and get to work!

- Decide how much time you will devote to this study session—then stick to your plan.

- Try not to take study breaks too frequently. If you're tired or bored, stand up and stretch for a few minutes, or do some quick jumping jacks to get your energy flowing again.

53.
Are you making the most of your study time? What do you already know? What don't you know? Try some of the following suggestions to get the most out of your study sessions.

- Read through your class and textbook notes.

- Go over old quizzes and tests.

- Go over previous homework assignments.

- Make review cards for each piece of information you have trouble remembering. Use 3" x 5" index cards and a pen or a marker to make the cards. Write a question about the material on the front of the card and the answer on the back.

- Go through the cards once. Put aside the cards as you learn the information on them. Spend more time on the concepts you have difficulty remembering. Review the material until you can easily go through all of the cards several times.

The area of a rectangle is length x width.

When was the Berlin Wall dismantled?

54. Make up practice tests for your Study Buddy and have him or her do the same for you. Take the test in pencil and see how well you do. Questions that you answered incorrectly should be studied again. Make up review cards for the material you cannot remember. Erase your answers to the test and take it again. Did your score improve?

55. Organize a study group of several students. Ask each student to write questions for an exam (in the same format in which the actual exam will be given, if possible). Collate all the questions into one practice test and give a copy of the test to each student in the group. Do the exams at home, then meet again to discuss the answers.

56. Explain to a parent, a brother or sister, or a neighbor the material you have studied. Try to present the concepts in clear, simple terms. Encourage your partner to ask questions if some of the information is not clear. Go back to your review cards or notes if you cannot answer his or her questions.

57. Teaching what you know is an excellent way to reinforce material you have learned. Help a classmate who is having trouble learning certain material. Teach a pretend class at home to your family. This can be done while studying for an upcoming test, or during one of your regular reviews.

58. Here are some tips for studying for a spelling test:

Tips

- Say each word aloud as you write it down three times.

- Close your eyes and try to spell the word.

- Think of two sentences using the word.

- Have a spelling bee with your Study Buddy.

- Ask a family member or friend to test you.

- If you repeatedly misspell a word while studying, try to think up a rhyme or trick to help you spell the word correctly.

59. Here are some tips for studying for a vocabulary test:

Tips

- Make a flash card for each vocabulary word. Write the word on one side and its definition on the other.

- Write five sentences using each word.

- Try to use each vocabulary word in conversation once a day. If some words are not likely to arise in everyday conversation, think of sentences while you travel to and from school.

- Use your vocabulary words to play a game of "Concentration" with your Study Buddy. Write down each word on a card and its definition on another card. Shuffle the cards together, then spread them out facedown on a flat surface. Turn over two cards at a time. If the word and definition match, keep the pair. If not, the next player goes. The person with the most matches wins!

60. Here are some tips for studying for a math test:

Tips

- Write out as many problems as you can using the skills that will be tested. The next day, answer the problems, then check your work. If any of your answers are wrong, figure out where you made mistakes. Study the concepts you didn't understand the first time, then take the test again.

- Make sure you understand *why* a formula works, or the logic of a particular math process. If you only know the steps you must take to get the answer but don't understand the reason, you may get fooled on a test. Also, it will be more difficult for you to understand upcoming units. You must have a clear knowledge of why easier math formulas work in order to understand the more difficult ones. If you are not sure of a concept being discussed in class, ask your teacher to spend a few more minutes explaining it until the concept is clear. If you are still unsure, ask a friend who understands the concept to explain it to you outside class.

- Exercise your math skills and improve your speed by trying to add, subtract, multiply, and divide things in your head. You can do this while you're in the supermarket or even playing a video game.

61. Think about what questions might be on the test. Ask yourself, "If I were the teacher, what kinds of questions would I use for this test?" Spend a few minutes brainstorming possible test questions. Chances are good that you'll come up with a number of the same questions your teacher will use on the actual test.

62. If you are preparing for an essay test and you are sure that a particular question will be asked, write a draft of your answer. Review the draft carefully and correct any mistakes. Look up additional information in your textbook, notes, and homework assignments that will make your essay better. Read your essay over and over until you have it memorized and can re-create it quickly. On test day, quickly jot down the basic points of your essay on your test paper. When the time comes to answer the question, you will have all your facts in front of you. Best of all, you will be able to spend more time on other questions.

63. For a multiple-choice or a true/false exam, use your notes to come up with questions that may be on the test. The items that you flagged or highlighted in your notes will probably make up many of the questions on the test.

64. Reward yourself after studying. You've worked hard and now you deserve a treat. Some ideas:

- Call a friend and chat about anything but the test.
- Have a bowl of ice cream.
- Watch a favorite television show.
- Take a long bike ride.
- Curl up with a good book or a magazine.
- Go out and look at the stars.

Sometimes thinking about the reward will help motivate you while you're studying!

65. Try to make sure the morning of the test will not find you scrambling around the house to get your stuff together. Gather all the materials you will need for the test the night before. Pack them up and leave them somewhere you will not forget them—by the door, on the kitchen table, strapped to your bicycle book rack.

66. Get a good night's sleep the night before the test. If you've studied some of the test material each day, you should not feel you have to cram the night before the test. The day of the test, get up a little earlier and eat a nutritious breakfast. Give yourself plenty of time for your morning routine—stay calm and relaxed!

67. Dress comfortably. You do not want to be worrying about how tight your jeans are or how much your new shoes are pinching your feet while taking an exam. All of your energy should be focused on the test.

68. Try to avoid talking about the exam to friends or classmates immediately before you take it. Any discussion may make you nervous or confuse you. Instead, take a deep breath and make sure you have a pen, a sharpened pencil, or any other material you will need to take the test.

Chapter 6

✓

It's Show Time!

69. It's normal to be a little nervous when you're about to take a test. However, if you are very, very nervous before a test, try to calm yourself by using this relaxation technique.

- Close your eyes and breathe in deeply.

- Hold your breath for a few seconds, then exhale.

Repeat this several times.

70. While you're waiting for the exams to be handed out, close your eyes and picture yourself in your favorite place—the beach, the ballfield, the movie theater. Then think about what you did the last time you were at this place, and what you'd like to do the next time you go there. Keep daydreaming until the teacher calls for everyone's attention.

71. When you receive your test, place it in a spot on the desk that does not force you to move your arm every time you read a question or write down an answer. If you are right-handed, place the exam on the left side of the desk and the answer sheet on the right. If you are left-handed, place the exam on the right side and the answer sheet on the left.

72. Listen to oral directions very carefully. If something doesn't make sense to you, be sure to ask the teacher to explain it again.

73. If the directions for the test are written on the test paper, be sure to read them very carefully—this is not the time to skim! Sometimes the directions change for each section, so proceed with caution. If you do not understand the directions, ask the teacher to clarify them.

74. Before you start answering the questions on a test, take a few minutes to write down information you think you might not remember later on. If there are some especially difficult math formulas, for example, jot them down at the beginning of the test and refer to them later if necessary.

75. Budget your time. Scan the test from beginning to end quickly. Estimate how much time you think it will take to complete each section. For example, you will need more time to answer essay questions than you will to do multiple-choice answers. Jot the time down next to each section. Use these estimates to pace yourself so you can complete the test.

76. Begin answering questions. WRITE NEATLY. This is especially important on short-answer or essay tests. If your teacher cannot read your writing, he or she may not give you any credit for your answer—even though it may be right!

Never write over an incorrect answer. If you decide you've made an error, cross out the incorrect answer. Write the correct answer above the incorrect one.

77. Make a check mark or a star next to any question you can't answer immediately. When you complete the test, go back to those questions and try to answer them. Sometimes you can pick up clues to difficult questions from other questions on the test.

78. If a question seems particularly difficult to understand, try underlining key words in the question. By focusing on these words, you may be able to figure out the main point. Or, try thinking out the question in your own words. You may be able to understand the question if you phrase it differently.

79. If you can't figure out the meaning of a question no matter how hard you try, raise your hand and ask the teacher to take a look. The question may have a missing word or may have been written unclearly.

80. CHECK YOUR ANSWERS! Try to leave five minutes or so at the end of any test to review your answers. Checking your test will often reveal careless errors.

1. 165	2. 304	3. 567	
x 68	x 94	x 23	
1320	1216	~~1711~~	1701
9900	27360	~~11340~~	11340
11,220	28,576	~~13,051~~	13,041

	32 r.19	177 r.6
4. 298	5. 64⟌2067	6. 32⟌5670
x 12	192	32
596	147	247
2980	128	224
3,576	19	230
		224
		6

81. Experts are divided about whether or not you should stick with your first answer no matter what. Use common sense. If an answer is obviously wrong, change it. Don't be afraid to change an answer that doesn't seem right upon your review. Often the very act of completing the test can shed new light upon a question that was asked earlier. Or, better yet, an answer may be given away in another question on the exam!

82. Don't panic if everyone else in the class seems to be furiously writing away. Everyone takes tests differently. For some people it's better to spend some time thinking about their answers before starting to write. Focus on your own test paper, and don't be distracted by those around you.

83. Don't worry if it seems as if everyone else in the class has finished and you still have a lot of answers to complete. Take as long as you need to do your best work. People who complete tests quickly do not always get the best grades.

84. DO NOT EVER, EVER CHEAT. You will lose respect for yourself, and your teacher and your classmates will lose respect for you as well.

Chapter 7
✓
All Kinds of Tests

85. Here are some tips for taking true/false tests:

- Watch for words that will try to divert you from the right answer. Extreme words like "all," "every," "always," and "only" exclude other options. These words are often found in false statements.

- Read the statement carefully. If one part is correct but another is wrong, the statement is false. All parts must be correct to be true.

• Watch for words like "usually" and "generally." These words are often found in true statements.

T____ F____ 1. Every United States president has had a college degree.

T____ F____ 2. The weather in Puerto Rico is generally mild.

Answers:

1. False. The extreme word "every" should have cautioned you.

2. True. The word "generally" in this statement is a clue that it is probably true.

86. Here are some tips for taking multiple-choice tests:

- Try to answer the question before looking at the answers. If your answer is one of those listed, mark it.

- Look for distractors. These are choices used to distract you from the correct answer. Read the questions and answers carefully and discard any distractors. Then decide which answer is correct from those remaining.

- Answers that are vague are usually distractors. Answers that are specific and detail-filled are usually the correct ones.

- Beware of answers that do not match grammatically with the question.

- Look for opposite answers among the choices. One of the opposite choices is often the correct answer.

- Remember—the answer is always right in front of you on a multiple-choice test.

1. Which president was in office when the Great Depression began?

a) Abraham Lincoln
b) John Kennedy
c) Herbert Hoover
d) Bill Clinton

2. This triangle is a _____ triangle.

a) equilateral
b) isosceles
c) right
d) scalene

3. During the early years of America, the Quakers supported

a) slavery.
b) taxes.
c) freedom for all people.
d) all of the above

Answers:
1. There are obvious distractors in these choices—Abraham Lincoln, John Kennedy, and Bill Clinton were all in office much earlier or later than the Depression.

2. The grammar in the statement indicates that the first letter in the answer must be a consonant. That means the first two choices are out.

3. Slavery and freedom are opposites, so the answer is probably one of these two choices.

87. Here are some tips for taking matching tests:

- Complete all the matches you are sure of on your first review of the exam.

- Use clues within the remaining items to make more matches.

- Look for clues, such as grammatical agreement, to try to solve more matches.

88. Here are some tips for taking completion tests:

- It is important to read the directions carefully. Determine if the teacher wants a one-word answer or a complete sentence or two.

- Look for grammatical clues, such as "a" or "an," or singular or plural agreement.

- After you fill in each answer, read the entire sentence to yourself to see if it sounds right.

- Even if you don't think your answer is exactly the right word or phrase the teacher is looking for, write it down. If you can't think of a better answer when you recheck your answers, you may still be given partial credit.

- Don't depend upon the length of the line to be filled in as a good clue for the length of an answer. A teacher may use a long line when looking for the answer "1776," or may use a short line when looking for the answer "where the first Olympics were held."

89. Here are some tips for taking essay tests:

- If you have a choice of which questions to answer, mark those you feel confident about. Write down on scrap paper anything you can think of that relates to those questions for use in your essays.

- Give yourself a time limit for each question and stick to it.

- Restate the question in your opening statement. Write one part of the answer in each paragraph and support it with details and facts.

- Summarize the main points of your essay in the last paragraph.

90. Be sure you understand the different terms that are used on essay questions. Here are some examples.

Analyze means you must explain the complexities of the question, and offer your opinion as well as experts' opinions.

—

Compare and contrast means you must describe similarities and differences.

—

Prove means you must take one side of a debate and show support for it with facts and details.

—

Diagram means you must draw a chart, a graph, or a picture.

—

Summarize means you must sum up key ideas and points without much detail.

—

Discuss means you must analyze the question and give in-depth description and detail about all sides of an issue or topic.

—

Give an example means you must choose one instance to support your argument or point.

—

Define means you must provide a clear, concise definition of the topic or situation.

—

Trace means you must give a narrative history of the topic.

91. When you have finished the essay questions you can answer easily, go back to the more difficult questions. If you are not sure about some of the parts of a question, try to avoid those issues in your essay.

92. Reread your essay answers after you have finished if time allows. Check for information you may have forgotten while writing, and for grammatical and spelling errors. You may lose points if your essay is not gramatically correct.

93. If you cannot finish an essay, at least write down an outline or as much information as you can. Any effort you make lets your teacher know that you have tried to do your best, and he/she might give you partial credit.

94. Here are some tips for taking math tests:

- Write down formulas or rules immediately. Use this information for quick reference as you go through the test.

- If you can't figure out a problem, try working it backward.

- Draw a picture to help you visualize a problem. For example, if you are working a geometry problem, it is sometimes helpful to make a quick drawing of the geometric figure to visualize the question.

- Restate a word problem in your own words. This will help you focus on the question being asked.

- Set up a word problem as a ratio or proportion.

Example:
The music store is selling 3 CDs for $10.00. How many CDs can Josh buy for $20.00?

Set this ratio up as a fraction, then cross-multiply to find the answer.

$$\frac{3}{10} \qquad \frac{x}{20}$$

10x=60
x=6
Josh can buy 6 CDs.

- To check your answers, reverse the procedure you used to find them.

Examples:

Addition

$$
\begin{array}{r}
72 \\
+68 \\
\hline
140
\end{array}
\qquad
\begin{array}{r}
140 \\
-68 \\
\hline
72
\end{array}
$$

Subtraction

$$
\begin{array}{r}
212 \\
-103 \\
\hline
109
\end{array}
\qquad
\begin{array}{r}
109 \\
+103 \\
\hline
212
\end{array}
$$

Multiplication

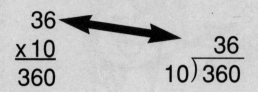

$$\begin{array}{r} 36 \\ \times 10 \\ \hline 360 \end{array}$$

$$10\overline{)360} \quad 36$$

Division

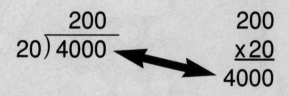

$$20\overline{)4000} \quad 200$$

$$\begin{array}{r} 200 \\ \times 20 \\ \hline 4000 \end{array}$$

Chapter 8

✓

Don't Let Your Guard Down

95. When you get a test back, review your teacher's comments. Do you think the comments are fair? Do you understand them? Ask your teacher for feedback if you do not. Make corrections on the test. File it properly in your study place.

96. Review each test with your Study Buddy or study group. Find out if many students missed the same questions. Analyze why. If a few students got the same question wrong, ask a student who understands the concept to explain it. If a large group of students did not understand the same question, ask your teacher to explain the concept and the answer. Your teacher will be happy to work with you until you fully understand the concept.

97. Look at an exam for clues to tell you about your test preparation. Did you make fairly accurate predictions about the types of questions that would be asked? Did you study the sections that were emphasized on the exam? Use these clues to better prepare for the next test.

98. Don't panic before a final! Before a midterm or final exam, retake all the previous exams for that class. Your old tests provide an excellent overview of all of the most important concepts discussed in class so far. Organize your study time based on the material you have already been tested on. You may find you need to go back to your notes and brush up on some of the material you learned at the beginning of the semester. If you have not yet been tested on the most recent information you've learned, you may need extra time studying these concepts. Chances are you will be able to quickly review your most recent tests, since much of that information is still fresh in your memory.

Many of the same questions that were asked on previous tests might be asked on the midterm or final, although they will probably be phrased differently. By going back to review old tests, you can save yourself hours of study time—and panic attacks!

99. Be diligent about your study habits. As you improve your method of studying, your test scores will also improve.

100. Constantly prepare for the next test. Keep to your daily and weekly study schedules so you can ace every test.

101. Reward yourself for a job well done! Whether you choose to rent a video or throw a post–final exam party for your entire class, remember that you've worked hard and you deserve this treat.

Appendix

Supply list

Keep these supplies neatly organized in your study place. If you need supplies that are not listed here, add them to the bottom of the list.

- ☐ pens
- ☐ pencils
- ☐ pencil sharpener
- ☐ lined paper
- ☐ graph paper
- ☐ file folders
- ☐ stapler
- ☐ paper clips
- ☐ globe
- ☐ atlas
- ☐ dictionary
- ☐ _____
- ☐ _____
- ☐ _____

- ☐ calculator
- ☐ correction fluid
- ☐ index cards
- ☐ highlighter
- ☐ almanac
- ☐ guidebooks
- ☐ encyclopedias
- ☐ manuals
- ☐ hole puncher
- ☐ bright light
- ☐ thesaurus
- ☐ _____
- ☐ _____
- ☐ _____

Some common symbols

Use these symbols in place of words when you take notes. Think of other symbols and add them to the bottom of the list.

☽	moon
♂	male/man/boy
♀	female/woman/girl
+	plus/positive
-	minus/negative
×	multiply
÷	divide
=	equals
$	money or dollars
#	number
&	and
?	question
●■▲▬●	circle, square, triangle, rectangle, oval
> / <	greater than / less than

_____   _____

_____   _____

_____   _____

_____   _____

_____   _____

_____   _____

_____   _____

Some common abbreviations

adj.	adjective
bio.	biology/biography
cent.	century
dept.	department
E/W/N/S	East/West/North/South
elec.	electricity
esp.	especially
F/C	Fahrenheit/Celsius
ft.	feet
govt.	government
incl.	including
inv.	invented/invention
is.	island
lat./long.	latitude/longitude
M	thousand
mi.	miles
orig.	originally
pic.	picture
pop.	population
Pres.	President
rev.	revolution
trans.	transportation
WWI/WWII	World War I/World War II

TEST LOG

Keep a separate test log for each subject. For each test, write the appropriate information on the lines provided. Keep this log in your test folder in your study place.

Grade_____

Subject _____

Teacher _____

Test Date   Material Covered   Grade

_____

_____

_____

_____

_____

_____

_____

_____

_____

_____

_____

Test Preparation Checklist

Use this helpful checklist before you take a test to make sure you are well prepared. If there are extra steps you take to prepare for a test, add them to the bottom of this list in the spaces provided.

❏ Place all study materials in your study place.

❏ If you need to research a topic (for example, a current events topic), make sure to complete the research well before the test date.

❏ Review and understand your notes, especially concepts the teacher stressed in his/her class discussions.

❏ Review and understand highlighted concepts in textbook.

❏ Review and understand in-class handouts.

❏ "Teach" material that will be on the test to a friend or parent; explain any concepts that are unclear.

❏ Prepare questions for practice test.

❏ Take practice test with Study Buddy; review and make corrections to test.

❏ Go over any difficult concepts with study group; share your practice questions.

❏ Ask teacher to explain concepts you don't understand.

- ☐ Write drafts for essay questions; memorize all major concepts.

- ☐ Memorize math/science formulas and rules that will be covered on the test.

- ☐ Prepare materials to bring to test (pen/pencil, compass, ruler, calculator, dictionary, etc.). Place these material in your backpack the night before the test.

- ☐ Get a good night's sleep the night before the test.

- ☐ _____

  _____

- ☐ _____

  _____

- ☐ _____

  _____

- ☐ _____

  _____

Bibliography

Flippo, Rona. *TestWise: Strategies for Success in Taking Tests*. Fearon Teacher Aids, 1988.

How to Study and Take Tests, Grades 5-8. Lee Canter & Associates, 1989.

Index

abbreviations, 27, 84
acronyms, 37
answers
     changing, 60, 61, 62
     checking, 61, 62, 71, 74, 75
assignment book, 30
assignments, 19, 22, 30, 34, 35, 36

cheating, 63

daydreaming
     as relaxation technique, 58
distractors, 67, 69
drugs, 16

eating healthily, 13–14, 54
essay questions
     definitions of terms, 73
     how to answer, 72
exercise, 16

files, 42
flash cards, 50
foods, 13
     chart, 14
formulas, 51, 59, 75

goal chart, 22–23

homework, 26, 34, 36, 46, 47

idea box, 28
inner time clock, 16, 17

library, 20, 22

mindmaps, 39
mnemonic devices, 37–39
monthly planner, 18, 30, 36

notes
    organizing, 29, 38–39
    reviewing, 35
    rewriting, 35
note-taking
    clues, 29
    highlighting, 29, 35, 39
    idea box, 28
    practicing at home, 27
    shorthand skills, 26–27
    tips, 26–27

reading, 40–41
    recalling information, 41
    scanning material, 40–41
reference books, 22

relaxation techniques, 57–58
review cards, 47, 48
rewards, 54, 81

scanning
    reading materials, 40–41
    tests, 59
sleep
    before a test, 15, 45, 54
    chart, 15
study
    breaks, 46
    buddy, 26, 34, 35, 36, 48, 49, 50, 80
    chart, 33
    cramming, 45, 54
    group, 48, 80
    habits, 26, 47, 81
    inner time clock, 16
    materials, 22
        for test day, 30–31, 54, 55
        organizing, 21, 46
    place, 20–21, 41, 79, 85
    scheduling time for, 17, 23, 33, 45, 80
    sign, 22
    supply list, 82
symbols, 83

teachers
    advice from, 26
    clues for note-taking, 29
    help from, 26, 30, 80

tests
    analyzing results, 42, 79, 80
    difficult questions, 60–61
    directions
      oral, 58
      written, 59, 71
    filing, 42
    log, 85
    practice, 48
    preparation for, 30, 31, 45–53, 80, 81, 86–87
    reviewing, 47, 79, 80
    scanning, 59
test-taking tips
    completion, 71
    essay, 53, 59, 60, 72–74
    matching, 70
    math, 51–52, 59, 75–77
    multiple choice, 59, 67–69
    spelling, 49
    true/false, 65–66
    vocabulary, 50
time
    budgeting when taking a test, 59, 72
    monthly planner, 18, 30, 36
    scheduling, 17, 23
    weekly planner, 18–19, 30, 36

Venn diagrams, 38

weekly planner, 18–19, 30, 36

Look for all the books in the

101

Ways

series

101 Ways to Do Better in School
0-8167-3285-X $2.95 U.S. / $4.25 CAN.

101 Ways to Get Straight A's
0-8167-3565-4 $2.95 U.S. / $4.25 CAN.

101 Ways to Boost Your Writing Skills
0-8167-3835-1 $2.95 U.S. / $4.25 CAN.

101 Ways to Boost Your Math Skills
0-8167-3836-X $2.95 U.S. / $4.25 CAN.

101 Ways to Take Tests with Success
0-8167-4225-1 $2.95 U.S. / $4.25 CAN.

101 Ways to Read with Speed and Understanding
0-8167-4226-X $2.95 U.S. / $4.25 CAN.

Available wherever you buy books.

Do you have a minute?

Then take the *One-Minute Challenge*. These books are packed with tricky challenges to test your basic skills in math, English, and vocabulary. With answers in the back of each book, these quizzes are a perfect primer for the SAT's. Earn better grades starting today!

One-Minute Challenges: Math
0-8167-4077-1 $2.95 U.S. / $4.25 CAN.

One-Minute Challenges: English
0-8167-4076-3 $2.95 U.S. / $4.25 CAN.

One-Minute Challenges: Vocabulary
0-8167-4227-8 $2.95 U.S. / $4.25 CAN.

One-Minute Challenges: Math and Reasoning
0-8167-4228-6 $2.95 U.S. / $4.25 CAN.

Available wherever you buy books.

Notes

Notes